AQUARIUM FISH
A PORTRAIT OF THE ANIMAL WORLD

Andrew Cleave

NEW LINE BOOKS

Fax: (888) 719-7723
e-mail: info@newlinebooks.com

Printed and bound in China

ISBN 978-1-59764-321-4

Visit us on the web!
www.newlinebooks.com

PHOTO CREDITS
Photographer/Page Number

E.R. Degginger 10, 11 (bottom), 14, 15, 18, 20, 22, 24-25, 26, 27 (top & bottom), 28 (top & bottom),
29, 30 (top & bottom), 31 (top and bottom) 32, 33, 34, 35 (top & bottom), 36-37, 38 (top & bottom),
39 (top & bottom), 40 (top & bottom), 41 (top & bottom), 42, 43, 44 (top & bottom), 45, 46 (top & bottom) 47

Tom Stack & Associates
Mike Bacon 54, 66
Gerald & Buff Corsi 52, 64-65
Dave B. Fleetham 12, 62
Gary Milburn 70 (top)
Randy Morse 6
Brian Parker 16, 21, 23, 55, 70 (bottom)
Mike Severns 50
Denise Tackett 7, 63
Larry Tackett 8-9, 13, 17, 71

The Wildlife Collection
Chris Huss 3, 4, 5, 11 (top), 19 (top), 48-49, 51 (top & bottom), 53, 56, 57 (top & bottom), 58, 59, 60, 61, 67, 68, 69
Dean Lee 19 (bottom)

INTRODUCTION

Who could dispute this fish's claim to being the queen angelfish, **Holacanthus ciliaris?** *The electric-blue markings of the juveniles are replaced by vibrant golds and yellows as the fish matures.*

Man has kept fish in captivity for almost as long as he has recorded history. The ancient Romans raised fish in ponds and tanks, though these creatures were destined not to be cared for as pets, but for the table. The city of Naples was noted for its elaborate system of ponds, both freshwater and marine, which were home to many large, and presumably edible, fish. It was probably the Chinese, however, who first kept ornamental fish, about one thousand years ago. Their favorite was the goldfish, which they kept in large bowls or opaque tanks (goldfish look attractive from above, so the lack of glass aquaria made little difference). The Japanese also enjoyed keeping goldfish, and perfected the art of breeding them in strange and beautiful colors.

By the middle of the seventeenth century goldfish had been introduced into Europe, but were still kept in bowls or ponds and viewed only from above. Many varieties were available, all of which looked interesting from above, with their bright colors, strangely shaped heads, and flowing fins; the more bizarre they appeared, they more popular they were.

By the middle of the nineteenth century, relatively cheap glass aquaria had been developed and more fish species were available to collectors. Amateur fish-keeping was still a somewhat expensive privilege of the upper classes, but many homes had one or two goldfish which they kept in bowls. Public aquaria were established in Britain and on the Continent, and some of the earliest books on the subject were published. And other fish-keeping techniques were invented in Britain to enable naturalists to keep cold-water marine species healthy for prolonged periods of study.

Toward the end of the nineteenth century, numerous species of tropical fish were brought to Europe and became extremely popular. Their great variety of colors and shapes, and the ease with which they could be kept, soon led them to become the most common fish collected in aquaria. Goldfish continued to be popular, but were more likely to be seen out of doors in ponds.

The earliest aquarists had quite a struggle to keep their pets alive without the benefit of electricity, thermostatically controlled heaters, efficient filtration systems, and the means to accurately test water for chemical imperfections. But the constant fascination of fish-keeping ensured that a consistent effort was made to find answers to these problems, so that today fish-keeping is a widespread and very popular hobby. Modern aquarists have a great deal of highly technical equipment available to them, and well over a hundred years of expertise and experience to draw on.

Today there is also an immense variety of fish available to the amateur aquarist. Tropical freshwater species are still the most popular, but cold-water aquarium fish like the goldfish, found in a great range of colors and forms, are still very widely kept. Saltwater aquaria present more problems than freshwater, but with the great advances in equipment design in recent years, tropical marine fish—plus organisms like anemones, prawns, and corals—can be kept by a reasonably skilled amateur. Cold-water marine species can be kept successfully, too, provided the correct equipment is available.

Once established, most aquaria require a minimum of upkeep and will enhance any room. A well-maintained aquarium with a healthy community of fish and a good growth of aquatic plants can also provide hours of interest and stimulus for further study; many interesting discoveries have been made by amateur aquarists pursuing their hobby. In fact, observing fish in an aquarium often leads to the even more rewarding study of fish in their natural environment.

These brightly colored maroon clownfish, or anemone fish, (Premnas biaculeatus), are one of several related species. All are similar in appearance and make an interesting addition to the smaller marine aquarium.

THE AQUATIC VERTEBRATES

Fish are classified as vertebrates—animals with backbones. One group, the sharks and rays, have skeletons made of cartilage, but all other fish have skeletons composed of bone. This supports the muscles and protects some of the organs, such as the brain and spinal cord.

Anatomy

The great bulk of the body of a fish is made up of muscle; the space occupied by internal organs is small compared to that of mammals. These muscles are used to flex the body from side to side to enable the fish to swim. It is the tail which provides propulsion; the smaller fins are used to stabilize the body and help the fish to steer and avoid danger. The dorsal fin, on the back, and the small pelvic and ventral fins on the underside, stop the fish rolling from side to side as it moves forward, and the paired pectoral fins at the front can be extended to help the fish stop quickly.

Most of the bony fish have a body covering of scales—thin, overlapping bony plates—which protect the skin beneath, help to streamline the body, and act as a flexible armor which enables the fish to be active without restricting its movement. In some fish the scales are very small, few in number, deeply embedded in the skin, or absent, but most species have a full body armor. The outer surface of a fish is covered with a layer of mucus, giving the fish a slimy feel. This mucus helps protect the body of the fish from external parasites or attacks by fungal diseases, and is also a further form of streamlining. It is very important when handling fish that the mucus not be wiped off, as this can leave the fish vulnerable to disease.

The mouths of fish are adapted to their way of life. Some have tiny mouths and no teeth, while others have large, gaping mouths and fearsome arrays of powerful teeth. Fish are unable to chew their food, but they can bite chunks from it, and some have tooth-like structures in their throats which help them grind up their meals.

The swim bladder—a gas-filled bladder deep inside the body—is a vital organ which acts as a buoyancy tank to help the fish

Following page: The Oriental sweetlips' (Plectorhynchus orientalis) large size and huge mouth hide the fact that this is a shy fish with the habit of eating only tiny morsels of food.

The long-nosed hawkfish, Oxycirrhites typus, is an agile predator, albeit of very small prey. Much of its time is spent motionless on suitable promontories from which it can dart out and snatch unsuspecting prey.

The tiny size and elongated shape of this diamond blenny, Malacoctenus boehlkei, enable it to take up residence in the most limited of spaces. These territories are valiantly defended against even the largest trespassers.

maintain its position in the water. Some species, particularly those which spend most of their time on the bottom, lack the swim bladder, and have some difficulty in swimming up to the surface. A few species can use their swim bladders to help produce grunting or clicking sounds.

Being permanently immersed in water, fish always run a risk of absorbing too much fluid. The kidneys, therefore, which are proportionately larger in fish than in other vertebrates, are also very important organs, responsible for maintaining the correct balance of water in the fish's body. A few specialized fish—particularly migrant species like eels and salmon—have kidneys which can cope with variable salinity, and so are able to live in both fresh and salt water, but these species are unsuitable for aquaria. Most fish are unable to make this switch; if they are put in the wrong type of water, they die very quickly.

Fish obtain oxygen through their gills, the red comb-like structures at the back of the mouth. Each fish has two sets of gills protected by bony flaps on either side of the head; when these are open it is sometimes possible to glimpse the gills inside them. Water, bearing dissolved oxygen, flows through the mouth and passes over the gills, where the oxygen is taken into the blood stream and carbon dioxide is released. The gills look red because they have a rich supply of blood vessels covered by a very thin membrane. As a fish swims along, apparently "drinking" water, it is really breathing by taking in a fresh supply of oxygen-rich water every time it opens its mouth. Some fish use this process to help them feed as well, filtering the water through much tougher, comb-like structures called gill rakers to remove tiny food particles or small organisms. A few fish can breathe by gulping air from the surface of the water into specialized organs which act like lungs; these species normally live in habitats where the water is very low in oxygen.

Environmental Adaptations

Fish are found in almost every type of watery habitat from the depths of the oceans, the open sea, and the seashore, to freshwater lakes, rivers, and ponds. They live in the coldest polar waters and the warmest tropical seas and rivers. Most require clean water, but some are tolerant of poor conditions and low oxygen levels. Fish exhibit many different adaptations to their habitats; while all have the same basic structures, there is a vast variety of shapes, sizes, and colors.

Fish of the open sea and those which live in large, fast-flowing rivers have what we think of as the classic fish shape: a well-proportioned body and a normal arrangement of fins. Many have rather plain coloring since they have no need for markings to camouflage them against a background. Many fish that normally spend their time swimming in open water can take food from the top or the bottom, simply by being good swimmers.

Those species that live on the bottom have flattened bodies with coloring that matches the surface they lie on, but their undersides, which remain hidden, are usually plain. Bottom-dwellers' mouths are directed downwards to facilitate feeding, and they often

This unusually named porkfish, Amisotremus virginicus, is part of a family of fishes commonly called grunts. By grinding their pharyngeal teeth, these fish are able to produce sounds audible to the human ear.

have barbels around the mouth to help them locate food in the mud below them. Fish that feed on the surface, however, have mouths designed to point upwards, so they can take in food without having to push too much of their body out of the water.

Fish that live in fast-moving rivers, such as trout, are often slender and streamlined to cope with the strong current. When put into an aquarium they become very restless, spending much of their time swimming rapidly around the tank. They also require high levels of oxygen and low temperatures,

Since its introduction to the aquarium trade, the scientific name of the ram, Microgeophagus ramirezi, has changed several times as a result of increasing knowledge of this delicate little fish's biology.

so may not be very suitable in a tank with other fish in it. Some fish that live in fast rivers, though, have flattened bodies to enable them to live on the bottom without being swept away by the current; these may be more suitable subjects for the aquarium.

Species that live in still water exhibit still other adaptations to their environment. While these types of fish are not in danger of being swept away by the current, they may be vulnerable to attacks by other fish, so camouflage is often quite important. Some have markings which look striking when isolated in an aquarium, but help the fish to blend in with surrounding vegetation in their natural habitat. Many fish have vertical stripes which make them attractive to the human eye, but these markings actually serve to help the fish merge visually with the stems of reeds or pond weeds. Likewise, fish with thin bodies can swim easily between plant stems, but when viewed from the side they have a distinctive appearance which makes them a good choice for an aquarium.

While camouflage is important to many fish, the need for cryptic markings is sometimes superseded by the need to attract a mate or warn off a rival. Fish that are able to escape from danger easily or ward off predators by attacking them can usually afford to have bright colors and striking body shapes. In some species, it is only the males which have the elaborate body forms or colors, while the females have more subdued markings. Many young fish lack the distinctive appearance of the adults. Because they are small and inexperienced, they need extra protection in order to survive; until they reach their full size they have markings which help them hide from danger. Although to human eyes some features may appear to be unnecessarily elaborate or extravagantly colored, they have developed that way over the course of thousands of years of slow evolution to suit the individual species and its way of life.

The large aquarium and continuous supply of live food required by fish such as this dragon moray eel, **Muraena pardalis,** *make keeping species like this a possibility only for enthusiastic specialists and public aquaria.*

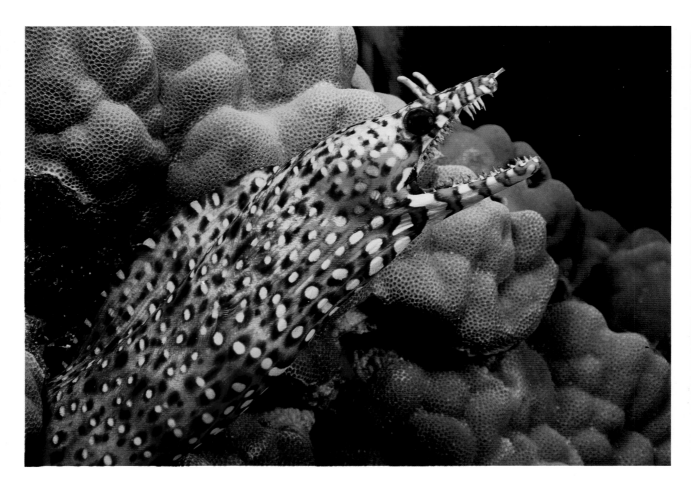

Senses

The fish's most important sense organ is the lateral line. In many species this can be seen quite clearly, looking like a line of dots running along either side of the body from head to tail. These dots are actually linked to sensitive nerve endings which are, in turn, connected to a fluid-filled canal beneath the skin. The lateral line is sensitive to pressure changes in the water, and helps the fish maintain an awareness of movement close to its body.

Most species are able to see well in color; in fact, fish themselves are often very colorful. They sometimes produce these colors to act as warnings or to attract mates, so their good color vision is therefore quite necessary to their survival.

The sense of smell is also very well developed in some fish, especially those which live in dark conditions or muddy water. Catfish, for example, have long, sensitive whiskers, and can find their food easily in the muddiest of water.

Reproduction

With a few exceptions, fish reproduce by laying eggs. Some species fertilize their eggs internally and the females carry the developing eggs inside their bodies, but most fish fertilize their eggs outside the body. Fish have paired reproductive organs inside their bodies which produce the sperm, or milt, in the males, and the eggs, or ova, in the females.

Mating, or spawning, often takes place as a group activity in shoaling fish species; vast numbers of eggs and sperm are shed into the water at once. Most of the eggs are fertilized, but some are eaten by the fish which produced them and any others in the vicinity. Fortunately, so many fertilized eggs are produced that many escape being eaten and hatch into tiny babies, or fry. Many of these are also eaten by fish and other predators, but once again, a few of the large number which hatch will escape predation and survive to become adults.

Once the eggs have been laid and fertilized, most species of fish take no further interest in

Gobies such as this elegant fire goby, Nemateleotris decora, share many similar habits with blennies, but there is no mistaking the gaudy colors that provide the gobies with perfect camouflage against the soft corals of shallow reefs.

them. Some fall to the riverbed and settle between stones or gravel, where they remain until they hatch, while others are sticky and adhere to plants or tree roots in the water. A few fish take more trouble with their eggs; these species usually lay far fewer than those which scatter them at random. Some make small nests to protect the eggs, and guard them until the young hatch; predators are warned away and the nest is kept clean. Other fishes' eggs are stuck to stones and watched over, and some even incubate the eggs inside their mouths. Once hatched, the fry are protected until they can fend for themselves; sometimes the parent keeps its young near the nest, or even shelters them inside its mouth.

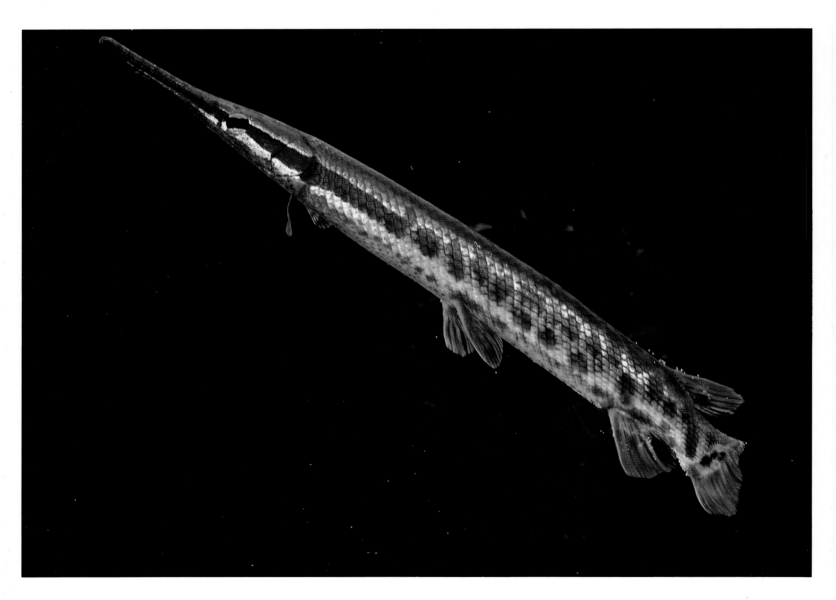

The body of the garpike, Lepisosteus osseus, *is heavily armored with thick scales, giving it a very primitive appearance. Indeed, fossil evidence suggests that these fish have remained unchanged for approximately 65 million years.*

With the skill and accuracy of a marksman, the archerfish, Toxotes jaculator, *is able to spit a jet of water at insects resting on leaves on (or even flying over) any body of water where these hungry predators reside.*

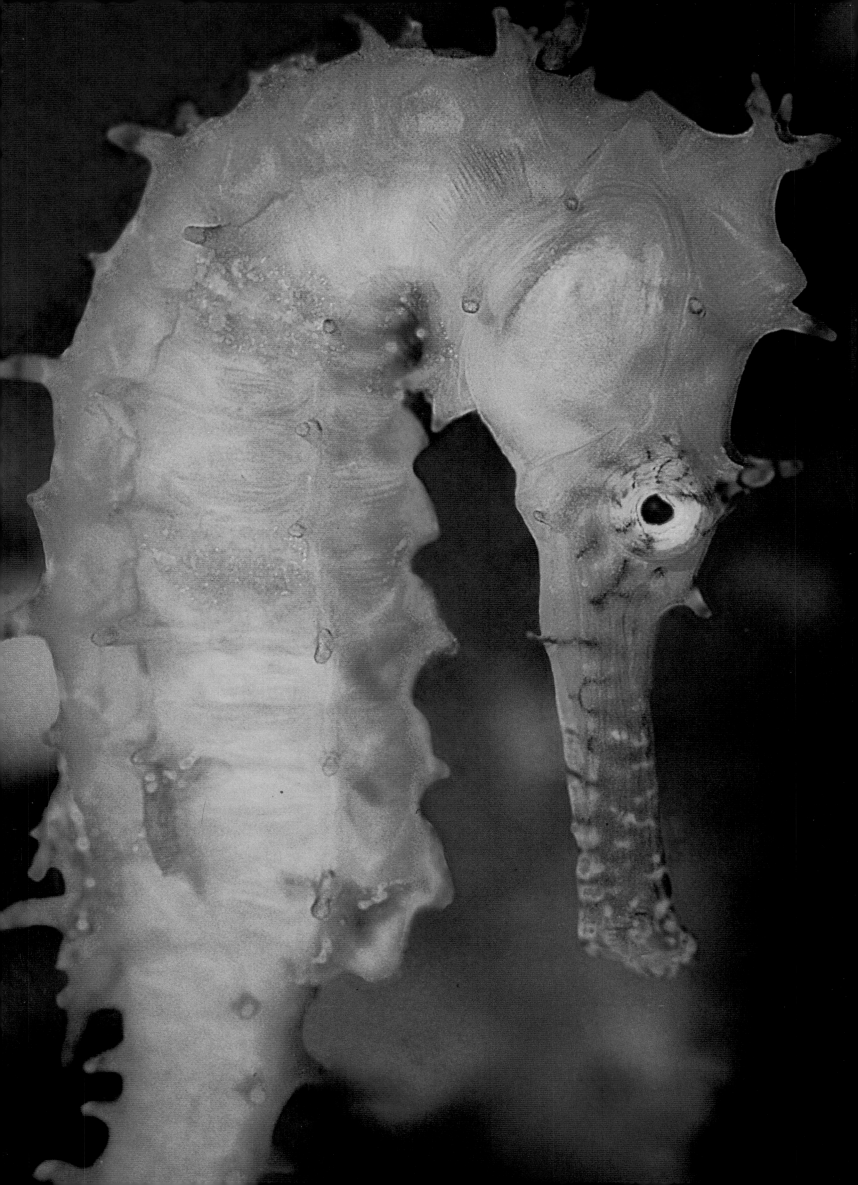

THE AQUARIUM: A WORLD IN MINIATURE

In their natural environment, most fish live in large bodies of water. Even a small pond is larger than the average home aquarium, so keeping fish in the artificial conditions of a small aquarium is likely to put them under stress unless the conditions are completely to their liking.

Setting Up An Aquarium

The first consideration should be the position of the aquarium. It should not be placed where it will get a lot of sun, because this can lead to overheating and a continuous, problematic growth of algae on the glass. In a shaded spot the lighting can be regulated and algal growth kept to a minimum. The tank should also be kept away from drafts, as these can cause temperature loss. Avoid, too, places where people may knock into the aquarium or where it becomes an obstruction.

A full aquarium is very heavy and needs a specially constructed stand. Even an average-size domestic aquarium weighs around 880 pounds (400 kilograms) when filled, so no

Despite their fragile appearance, seahorses, Hippocampus reidi, make surprisingly hardy aquarium occupants when kept with similarly peaceful species. Under the right conditions, it is not unusual for them to breed in captivity.

Only when this firefish, Nemateleotris splendida, is confident it has a safe hole to retreat to, will it take on the flame-red coloration that gives the species its name. If a suitable site is not provided in the aquarium, this fish will busily set about making its own.

This half-masked cory, **Corydorus ambiacus,** *is representative of a group of catfish that, without question, are the most popular kept in captivity. Their small size and peaceful nature make them the ideal occupants for the bottom layers of any community aquarium.*

ordinary shelf or piece of furniture is strong enough. (Be sure, too, that the floor beneath the stand is sturdy.) A stand which incorporates some storage space beneath it is very useful for housing pumps and filters, food, and cleaning equipment.

It also is important that the aquarium has its own electrical socket to supply the lighting, heater, and filters. These should not be unplugged at any time, so a socket which also has to supply other appliances may not be safe.

The aquarium should, if possible, be made entirely of glass; metal structures corrode easily in constant contact with water. A marine aquarium should have no metal parts

at all, as sea water is extremely corrosive. Choose equipment from a reliable dealer and follow his or her guidance as to how the tank should be set up.

Only purchase fish from a reputable dealer. It should be obvious by observing them in the dealer's tanks if the fish are alert and healthy. Ask to watch the fish feeding; if they show no interest in food they may not be healthy. And be sure that the aquarium is ready to receive fish and has been properly established before they are taken home; all lights, filters, and other equipment must be in working order before any fish are introduced.

In its natural environment this Moorish idol, Zanclus canescens, is a peaceable schooling fish of relatively open water. It requires a huge amount of swimming space; as a result, it often proves very temperamental and difficult to keep in the confines of an aquarium.

Some aquarists have a morbid fascination for venomous fish, but considering the lion fish's marvelous coloration and bold indifference to its surroundings, it is not difficult to see how the Pterios volitans *has become so popular.*

The Marine Aquarium

Keeping fish in a marine aquarium can be a very difficult task. Maintaining the correct salinity of the water is very tricky, and providing high enough oxygen levels in a well-stocked tank is also a challenge.

The great majority of marine fish kept in aquaria are tropical species which, in the wild, inhabit coral reefs. The reef provides very stable environmental conditions, so these fish are rather intolerant of fluctuations. On the reef, oxygen levels are always high and the light is very bright, as coral grows only in very shallow, clear water. Temperatures are constant and the water is kept in good condition, free from waste, by the constant flow of fresh seawater.

Seawater is highly corrosive, so the tank must be made entirely of glass or plastic, with no metal parts at all. (Metal not only corrodes badly, but also dissolves in the water, poisoning the fish, even in small quantities.) While marine fish are less inclined to jump out of the tank than freshwater fish, there is a risk that contaminants may drop in, so the tank must be covered very carefully. This will also help control evaporation; as water evaporates the salinity increases, so the tank must be topped off with distilled water.

Very bright lighting is also important in a marine aquarium. This encourages the growth of algae, which helps to remove some of the waste from the fish and is in turn eaten by the fish. Seawater is a complex mixture of salts at a concentration of approximately 3.5 parts per thousand. The largest constituent is sodium chloride, or common salt, but many other salts, in lesser amounts, are also present. It used to be very difficult to make artificial seawater because of the great number of trace elements present, but now excellent synthetic seawater can be made by mixing commercially prepared salts with tap water.

Seawater is alkaline, but in an aquarium there is a tendency for it to become slightly acidic due to the build up of organic waste and the higher levels of carbon dioxide. Nitrogen levels can also build up in the

This unusual looking elephant-nosed fish, **Gnathonemus petersii***, from central Africa, is one of a huge variety of electric fishes. The small electrical field this fish produces around its body varies according to the fish's level of stress. Scientists are exploring the commercial value of this species as an indicator of pollution in freshwater rivers and lakes.*

closed conditions of an aquarium, so the water must be tested regularly and filtration needs to be very efficient. Biological filters, in which a colony of bacteria break down waste drawn into the gravel, are very effective, provided the current is strong enough to constantly draw waste down into the gravel. External filters are sometimes used in addition to biological filters; these help to maintain very clean conditions.

In the marine aquarium, a foamy scum usually builds up on top of the tank; this scum is like the albumen in eggs, removed by bacteria in the wild. A protein skimmer, powered by an air pump, can be used to remove this surface layer from the aquarium. Despite the difficulties of maintaining water quality, once a routine has been established to test the water regularly and scrupulously remove any dead or waste material, an established tank with the correct balance of fish and other creatures will remain trouble-free for very long periods.

If about one quarter of the water in the tank is changed every two months or so, being replaced with freshly made artificial sea water, the community can continue indefinitely.

Breeding Fish at Home

Breeding fish in captivity requires more skill on the part of the aquarist than does simply keeping them in good condition. Breeding is often stimulated in the wild by a change in the seasons, such as an increase in the length of daylight or a rise in water temperature in the spring. Fish also need to be in peak condition in order to breed successfully, therefore it is important for the aquarist to know a good deal about the life and habits of the fish in their natural habitat and to watch for the signs of readiness to breed among the captive fish. In the confines of an aquarium it is very likely that the eggs will be eaten, so it is preferable to provide a separate tank for spawning to allow them to hatch in safety.

The nocturnal habits and predatory behavior of the longjaw squirrelfish, **Holocentrus marianus,** *do not make them the most popular of marine aquarium specimens. Nonetheless, their shoaling activity and red color can make a specialist tank containing six or more of the fish a truly spectacular sight.*

The Arowana, **Osteoglossum bicirrhosum,** *can reach an awesome size; only very young specimens can be kept in aquaria. Take on the responsibility of these giants only if you can provide them with the space they require to grow.*

Pipefish, Syngnathus grisseolineatus, *make wonderful additions to small, calm aquariums. Provided there are lots of hiding places among algae and an almost constant supply of small, live food, they will continue to thrive for many years.*

FAMILIES OF FRESHWATER FISH

The Cyprinids are the familiar carp family, containing many common species of fresh-water river fish such as carp, bream, roach, and tench. Goldfish—the first true aquarium fish—are Cyprinids, but now about three hundred other species of Cyprinid are also kept by aquarists. In all there are about 1,500 species in this family, found around the world except in Australia and Antarctica. Most species come from rivers, so they are rather active in a still-water aquarium where there is no strong current to swim against. Many Cyprinids are shoaling fish and will not thrive if kept singly.

Cyprinids
There is a great range of sizes and shapes in this family, from tiny barbs at only 3/4 inch (2 centimeters) long, to the magnificent Indian mahseer at over 6 1/2 feet (2 meters) (although this is most certainly not an aquarium fish). The typical member of this family has an elongated body with large scales and a conventional arrangement of fins. The sexes normally look alike except when the females are ready to spawn and are full of roe, making them look more rounded. Cyprinids' mouths, which often have barbels at the sides, can be quite large, and some have a few blunt teeth in the throat to grind food.

Barbs are widespread warm-water Cyprinids found across Africa and Asia. They need high levels of oxygen and are lively swimmers. Many of them take well to life in an aquari-

The underslung mouth of the red-fin shark, **Labeo erythrurus**, *has lips that have evolved into sucking organs, within which are rows of horny teeth. Unlike the true shark, this small, freshwater fish feeds by using its specially adapted mouth to rasp algae off rocks.*

um and can usually be encouraged to breed under the right conditions. Rasboras are found in Malaysia and Indonesia; there are about thirty species. These are small, fast-swimming fish which live in shoals and prefer fast-flowing water. It is somewhat difficult to encourage rasboras to breed, as they require acidic water and readily eat their eggs as soon as they have been released.

Danios are Cyprinids found on the Indian subcontinent as well as in Sri Lanka and Burma. They are tolerant of a wider range of conditions and are relatively easy to breed. These are surface feeders and quite active in the aquarium.

Goldfish, **Carassius auratus,** *are incredibly tolerant of poor water quality, a trait which is often misinterpreted as meaning that these fish are easy to keep in aquariums. However, a large aquarium with consistent water conditions is essential for these fish to thrive in captivity.*

The brilliant metallic red of this male rosy barb, Barbus conchonius, is only this intense when the fish is in breeding condition. Otherwise the species remains a less exciting, but nonetheless attractive, silvery color.

The bizarre-looking pearl scale Carassius auratus, is classified as exactly the same species as the common goldfish. Its appearance is a result of years of selective breeding to accentuate its interesting features.

Fancy varieties of goldfish such as this red-cap oranda, Carassius auratus, *are often less tolerant of fluctuations in water conditions than the normal varieties and, as such, are not a good idea for anyone new to fish-keeping.*

Perfectly adapted to its life in the fast-flowing streams of Southeast Asia, the pearl danio, Brachydanio albolineatus, *also thrives in aquaria where this sort of swirling turbulence, recreated by modern power filters, is provided.*

Characins

Many very popular and well-known species of aquarium fish are Characins. It is a very large and diverse family, diplaying a wide range of adaptations to varied conditions in freshwater. Most are found in the rivers of Central and South America, especially the Amazon, but a few species live in North America and in northern Africa.

Size and body shape can vary widely; some Characins are flattened laterally for swimming between plant stems, while others are elongated and have round bodies designed for fast swimming against strong currents. Male Characins have a very tiny hook at the tip of the rays on the anal fin, and a few species have hooks on other fins as well; this is a useful guide to the sexes when attempting to breed Characins. If Characins are caught in a very fine mesh net small males may cling to the net momentarily.

Unlike the Cyprinids, Characins have teeth; the most striking example is the notorious piranha. Not all varieties have such large teeth, however; many have smaller and more numerous teeth. Fish that have teeth are most likely to be carnivorous, feeding on organisms smaller than themselves. In the aquarium they appreciate live food such as daphnia or tubifex, but they can also live on high-quality dried foods.

Between the dorsal fin and the tail of Characins is a small, fleshy adipose fin which has no fin rays (this feature is also found in members of the salmon family). The function of this fin is not clear. There are a few Characins which do not conform to this standard pattern: They have lost the adipose fin as well as their teeth.

If an attempt is made to breed Characins, they must be given live food, but this is a very difficult group to raise in captivity. Commercial breeders raise Characins, but those reared from several generations in captivity are usually far less striking than their wild counterparts. There is less competition in the aquarium, so the need for bright coloration is reduced and the captive stock

With its large size and primarily vegetarian feeding habits, this banded leporinus, Leporinus fasciatus, will make short work of any soft, feathery leafed plants in the aquarium. Supplement this fish's diet with frozen spinach, and decorate its aquarium with only the hardiest of plants.

The striking black coloration of this delightful tetra is the only similarity the black widow, Gymnocorymbus ternetzi, *has with its deadly arachnid namesake. Its peaceful, shoaling activity will liven up any well-planted community aquarium.*

The bulging chest of the silver hatchetfish, Gasteropelecus levis, *encloses muscles that power the long pectoral fins found in this family. These muscles are used for a powered "flight" across the surface of the water, enabling the fish to escape would-be predators.*

Like many tetras, this cardinal tetra, Cheirodon axelrodi, is happiest in a shoal. Their vivid blue and red colors intensify if these fish are kept in a well-planted aquarium filled with soft water.

The red spot on the side of this bleeding-heart tetra, Hyphessobrycon erythrostigma, demonstrates how the fish got its name. Its subtle coloring can add a refreshing contrast to an aquarium containing a lively shoal of vividly colored tetras.

gradually becomes less attractive in appearance. Nonetheless, it is preferable to breed the fish in captivity rather than continually catching them in the wild. Not only is it bad conservation practice, but there is also a greater risk of introducing diseases when fish are taken from rivers.

The tetras are the most popular species in this large family. There are only two genera—*Hyphessobrycon* and *Hemigrammus*—which are true tetras, but, unfortunately, most other small Characins are given this name as well. Taxonomists have attempted to correct the nomenclature, but aquarists still call a wide variety of fish tetras.

Cyprinodonts

This family is also known as egg-laying toothcarps or killifish. They are widespread across most of the tropics, though they are not found in Australia or the East Indies. The natural habitat of most toothcarps is small pools with plenty of vegetation. The water is often very acidic as a result of the build-up of decaying plant material, so keeping these fish in an aquarium requires very special conditions. Although they may be compatible with other fish in terms of behavior, few other species can tolerate the acid water conditions, so toothcarps are usually kept in single-species tanks.

Most toothcarps have cylindrical bodies designed for fast swimming, with the dorsal and anal fins positioned far back. The tail is frequently deeply forked, a further adaptation to fast swimming. Most species have a large mouth, typical of predators, but they can usually be kept with other fish provided they are not much smaller than the toothcarps.

Toothcarps are usually small and elongated and best suited to surface feeding. Insects are frequently taken, but they also feed on small fish. Dried food is not very popular with

The bold yellow and black markings of this golden julie, Julidochromis ornatus, *stand out well against an aquarium furnished with an abundance of dark-colored rocks. This type of aquarium decor will also provide this species with the numerous retreats it requires.*

them in the aquarium, so frequent meals of live food are necessary.

Some toothcarps, such as the egg-buriers, have very strange life cycles. They live in temporary pools which are subject to rapid drying, so they must lay eggs which are resistant to drought. These fish rely on sudden rain storms to fill their pools, stimulate the eggs to hatch, and enable them to feed, grow, and complete their life cycle in a very short time before the pool dries up once more.

The live-bearing toothcarps give birth to live young; this is possible because the fertilized eggs are retained inside the female's body until they have hatched. These species are confined to the Americas, and live in freshwater, brackish water, and, very occasionally, the sea itself. The females are generally larger than the males, and when carrying developing eggs become very fat. Males have a specially adapted anal fin which allows them to deposit sperm inside the female; this usually follows a frenzied courtship display, with the tiny male doing his utmost to interest a normally disinterested female.

If mated in captivity the females must be left completely undisturbed, as they will readily abort their brood. Once fertilized, however, the female can produce several broods from one deposit of sperm. The brood is usually very small, and the tiny young are able to start feeding as soon as they are born. The live-bearing toothcarps are quite tolerant of a wide range of conditions in the aquarium, and, if kept in good condition, they will breed quite freely.

Cichlids

This important group of freshwater fish is found over a wide area, ranging from the southern United States and Central and South America to Africa, the Middle East, India, and Sri Lanka. Aquarists, however, are most interested in the species from Africa and the Americas.

The African cichlids are comparatively small and come from a variety of habitats. West African species usually live in acid waters where there is a lot of vegetation. East African species, most of which are found in Lake Malawi, come in a wonderful range of colors, many of them rivaling marine species. The size and varied conditions of the lake have given rise to an immense variety of

species, most of which are small and strongly territorial. They require hard, alkaline water with salt added to it. Several other East African lakes have populations of cichlids as well; since they normally inhabit these large lakes, they are rather slow moving in the aquarium.

The American cichlids are also very numerous and varied, although only the smaller species, commonly known as dwarf cichlids, are likely to be kept in the aquarium. These are suitable for community tanks, only becoming aggressive towards other fish when breeding.

Cichlids have many physical characteristics similar to their relative the common perch, particularly the large, spiny-rayed fins. Body shape can vary from streamlined and elongated to rounded, and sometimes flattened. All of the species have spiny fins and a lateral line divided into two parts.

Cichlids are best kept by specialists who are interested in them for their breeding behavior and color changes. These are predatory fish and have strong teeth, so they are usually kept in single-species aquaria. A few live in shoals, but when they reach breeding condition they become territorial and drive other fish away. Most have aggressive habits and will disturb the gravel, uprooting plants, so

The tapering snout of this butterfly fish, Pantodon buchholzi, disguises an otherwise enormous mouth that is ever ready to engulf anything that passes by. In the aquarium these fish often prove difficult to feed, requiring a ready supply of suitably sized live food.

their tanks can not easily be kept in an attractive condition.

If cichlids are introduced to a tank as immature fish they will not be aggressive toward each other, but if two adults are introduced they will fight furiously. Separating them by a sheet of glass until they become tolerant of each other often works. Adults can be brought to breeding condition by giving them plenty of live food and keeping the temperature of the tank a little warmer than normal. They can be encouraged to breed by placing them in a large tank without plants but with a good selection of rocks, upturned flowerpots, or driftwood. Many breed in caves, so if the materials in the tank are

Following page: Named after a famous boxer, the Jack Dempsey, Cichlasoma octofasciatum, deserves its name. In the aquarium, it is incredibly pugnacious and should not be kept with any other fish.

In the calcium-rich waters of Lake Tanganyika, these Brichards' cichlids, Lamprologus brichardi, form part of a massive community of similar fish species holding territories among the boulders. Although unsuitable for a normal aquarium, Brichards' cichlid makes a peaceful addition to a community of related species.

This zebra angelfish's (Pterophyllum scalare) laterally compressed shape and vertical stripes are perfect adaptations to living in the weedy, slow-moving rivers of South America, where it is able to hide among tree roots and prey on invertebrates and small fish.

The discus, Symphysodon aequifasciata, is a very delicate fish that does not adjust instantly to aquarium conditions. It is often viewed as the ultimate challenge to many freshwater fish-keepers.

arranged in such a way as to form good hiding places these will be readily used.

If conditions meet with their approval a pair of adults will choose a nesting site and carefully clean it of all debris. The sticky eggs are guarded until they have hatched, and the young are watched very carefully as they take their first few meals. As long as the adults are not disturbed they will look after the young quite well, but it may be necessary to remove some of them to a separate tank if there are

signs of their being eaten. The fry need to be raised on a diet of live food such as brine shrimp and daphnia. Adults are eager feeders, taking not only live food, including large items like earthworms, but also dried food and some plant material.

Anabantidae

This group is more commonly known as labyrinth fish because of a special organ they possess which enables them to breathe air from the surface. As a result of this ability they are very adaptable, and can live in conditions which would kill other fish. Siamese fighting fish are a very well known species of labyrinth fish, as are gouramis and climbing perches.

The labyrinth organ is made up of a series of bony plates covered with thin tissues set inside cavities on either side of the head. This creates a large surface area through which oxygen can be absorbed. Some labyrinth fish are so dependent on this method of breathing that they will die if they are not able to reach the surface and take in air; they make regular trips to the surface, normally about three times a

Many cichlids show a degree of parental care which sets them apart from many other fish species. This brightly colored Lake Nyasa cichlid, Pseudotropheus elongatus, takes parenthood so seriously that it broods its newly hatched young in its mouth.

The spectacular colors and long fins of the Siamese fighting fish, Betta splendens, are instantly recognizable to both hobbyists and other male fighting fish. If two males are placed together, these fish will instantly set about proving how they got their name.

Like many of the fish that give birth to live young, the swordtail, Xiphophorus helleri, is easy to breed in captivity. Unfortunately, its readiness to breed with the closely related platies, Xiphophorus maculatus, has resulted in a mish-mash of non-specific variations being available in the trade.

Although incredibly popular with many newcomers to fish-keeping, the black mollie, Poecilia latipinna, *is not the easiest of fish to keep healthy in the aquarium. It does best in a tank to which a small amount of sea salt has been added.*

The blue gourami, Trichogaster trichopterus, *is one of many variations of this species available in the aquarium trade. Looking at this specimen, it is difficult to see how this fish got its other common name, three-spot gourami.*

The small size, bright colors, and tolerance of a variety of conditions have made the fancy guppy, **Poecilia reticulata**, a favorite with hobbyists for decades. An easy fish to breed in captivity, this species has been selectively bred to produce variations in tail size, shape, and color.

The dwarf gourami, **Colisia lalia**, is an incredibly hardy little fish and will readily breed in captivity. The male constructs a floating bubble nest out of saliva and pieces of plant debris, and guards it against any potential threat.

minute, in order to release a bubble of used air and take in a fresh supply. Newly hatched fish breathe in the normal way, through their gills, but after a few weeks, when they increase in size, they need to supplement their oxygen intake with the aid of the labyrinth.

Labyrinth fish have remarkably flexible bodies, with all the internal organs compressed into a small space near the head. Most are aggressive, especially when breeding, and are best kept away from other species.

This group has a unique method of caring for their eggs: The male produces a raft of bubbles, releasing mucus from his mouth to bind them together. Sometimes pieces of floating plant material are incorporated into the bubble nest to help strengthen it.

Males have a very elaborate courtship display and can become quite aggressive toward females if they do not respond favorably. A non-responsive female may not be ready to

In the wild the brilliant colors of the male guppy, Poecilia retiiculata, *are aimed at enticing the females to breed. In adopting this strategy, the male guppy makes himself far more obvious to predators than the well-camouflaged female.*

The beautifully marked pearl gourami, Trichogaster leeri, *is slightly more delicate than its hardy relatives. Its trailing, filamentous fins can encourage antisocial fin nipping in otherwise peaceful community fish such as barbs.*

The unusual, transparent body of the glass catfish, Krypopterus bicirrhus, *with its visible internal organs and skeleton, makes this fish very popular as a novelty.*

Many killifish, such as this lace-finned species, Pterolebias zonatus, *have a very short life cycle and, once they have spawned, they will often die. This curious situation is an extraordinary adaptation to living in the shallow pools of the tropics, which dry up with the change of seasons.*

spawn, so she needs somewhere to hide from the male, preferably among thickly planted vegetation. If the female is receptive she will remain near the male's bubble nest, and he will turn her upside down by wrapping himself around her. Once the eggs are released, the male fertilizes them, draws them into his mouth, and then squirts them into the nest; in some species the female helps him do this. The male may try to mate with the female again if all of her eggs were not released the first time, but once the pair is done the male drives the female away.

After mating, the male remains on guard, retrieving any eggs that fall out of the nest and jetting them back into the bubbles with his mouth. He also watches out for any young which escape from the nest and ensures that they are safely returned. The newly hatched young are very difficult to rear, requiring minute live food and warm water, but once they have matured they are very hardy.

Catfish

Catfish are characterized by having sensory barbels around the mouth which enable them to find food on the bottom of muddy rivers and lakes. There are about two thousand species of catfish, all of which are very varied. They can be found in a number of different types of habitat, from clear, fast-flowing mountain streams to slow-moving and sometimes stagnant waters. Many are resis-

The long barbels around the mouth of this polka-dot, or pim pictus, catfish, **Pimelodus pictus,** *have very sensitive taste cells at their tips, enabling the fish to find food in the murkiest of waters, even at night.*

tant to unpleasant conditions which would kill other fish.

Some catfish have sucker-like mouths which enable them to browse on algae or cling to stones in very fast currents. A few species are aggressive and predatory, but most are quiet scavengers who stay near the bottom searching for food. Some are nocturnal feeders, remaining hidden during the day.

The legendary red-tailed catfish, **Phractocephalus hemioliopterus,** *has the potential to reach an enormous size in the aquarium, and will eat anything it can fit into its mouth. They are only suitable for enthusiasts who can accommodate these greedy monsters.*

Cobitidae

The Cobitidae, or loaches, are quite widespread; they can be found across Europe and throughout Asia and North Africa. They bear a superficial resemblance to the catfish, having barbels around the mouth. In the wild loaches prefer fast-flowing rivers, and spend most of their time sheltering among stones waiting for food to be swept towards them. They have no visible scales on the body, which is usually elongated and eel-like.

Loaches require high levels of oxygen; some supplement what they obtain through their gills by gulping down a mouthful of air from the surface from time to time. Waste gases leave the body through the vent. Loaches can detect changes in atmospheric pressure, and become restless when the weather is about to change; one species, known as the weatherfish, has been kept as a form of living barometer for centuries.

Most loaches appreciate a diet of live food, although they are unable to catch fast-moving prey. They are good burrowers, constantly snuffling through the gravel in search of a meal.

Often seen as juveniles in aquarium stores, the somewhat temperamental clown loach, **Botia macracantha,** *has the potential to reach a surprisingly large size in captivity; in very large aquaria these attractive fish can reach 12 inches (30 centimeters) in length.*

It is said that the weather loach, **Misgurnus anguilicaudatus,** *is sensitive to changes in barometric pressure and can predict the coming of a storm with frantic swimming, a marked change from this fish's normally peaceful behavior.*

FAMILIES OF MARINE FISH

A great number of families of marine fish are found in the world's seas and oceans, but only a few of them are suitable for keeping in an aquarium. Many live only in the deepest oceans or grow to an immense size, while others are such specialized feeders that it is impossible to keep them healthy in captivity. Only those families which are easily obtained and thrive in captivity are described here.

Chaetodontidae

The Chaetondontidae, or butterfly fish, are attractive, reef-dwelling fish of tropical seas. They typically have flattened bodies and spiny dorsal fins. Their mouths are usually tiny and beak-like so they can pick out morsels of food from crevices in the reef. A number of species are very specialized feeders, living in association with a particular species of coral, and are not easy to keep in

The false eye spots on the flanks of the four-eye butterfly fish, Chaetodon capistratus, *act as a decoy to confuse potential predators. As a result of this bit of visual deception, the fish is able to flee from an attack in the opposite direction to that anticipated by its predator.*

This ornate coralfish, Chaetodon ornatis-simus, *inhabits the outer reefs of Hawaii and the western Pacific where it swims freely with its own and other, closely related species. In the aquarium, however, this species can be pugnacious and completely intolerant of other fish.*

With its upper and lower jaws extended into a needle-sharp point, this brilliantly colored long-nosed butterfly fish, Forcipiger flavissimus, *certainly has an advantage when it comes to picking tiny morsels of food from between coral heads on the reefs where it resides.*

The submissive, head-down posture of this raccoon butterfly fish, Chaetodon iunuia, *is part of a ritualistic display performed by all fish when receiving the services of the cleaner-wrasse.*

the aquarium. Most, however, are fairly tolerant of other fish and can live in a well-heated aquarium with high salinity. So far, butterfly fish have not been bred in captivity, but when given a good, varied diet with plenty of live food they can be kept in healthy condition.

Labridae

The wrasse family is a large and widespread group comprising about six hundred species, several of which live in the cold waters around the shores of northwestern Europe. They are strong swimmers with elongated, muscular bodies; they propel themselves forwards with powerful movements of their pectoral fins, and can dive down to the bottom to dig into gravel quite easily. Some small species will actually bury themselves in the sand at night, and many will hide in the gravel when first introduced to a new tank.

Aquarists not familiar with the habits of the wrasse may be surprised to see a large fish lying on its side on the bottom of the tank in a deep sleep. A coating of mucus is sometimes secreted to cover and protect the body at night.

All of the species have strong teeth and jaws which they use to crush the shells of mollusks and crustaceans. They eat a variety of foods, but prefer that which they can literally sink their teeth into. Once they have settled into an aquarium wrasse become relatively bold and can be fed easily, but they require special care for the first few days.

In the wild, it is not uncommon for wrasse such as this harlequin wrasse, **Lienardella fasciata,** *to change their sex. Normally the dominant females of a single-sex group undergo this role reversal and, invariably, the largest, most colorful fish are males.*

Four-spot butterfly fish, **Chaetodon quadrimaculatus,** *are relatively small and may lack confidence in an aquarium containing larger, more boisterous fish. As a result, they tend to spend much of their time hiding and miss out in the rush for food.*

Despite being almost exclusively carnivorous, these rainbow wrasse, Cheillinus undulatus, are surprisingly tolerant of other fish species. Their elongated bodies and dazzling colors make them an interesting addition to any marine community.

The coloration of this huge, adult Spanish hogfish, Bodianus rufus, *bears little resemblance to the smaller blue and yellow specimens often seen in aquarium shops. Like many wrasse, the juveniles of this species will often perform cleaning services for other fish in the aquarium.*

Pomacentridae

This family includes the damselfish and the clownfish, both very popular with marine aquarists. They are very hardy in the aquarium and seem to be tolerant of a range of conditions. Most are very easy to feed, taking a wide range of foods, and do not grow to a great size, so several can be kept in a moderate-size tank. They are more tolerant than most reef fish of a build-up of nitrites in the water, so they are sometimes used to help prepare a tank for other more sensitive inhabitants: The nitrogenous waste they release helps to build a bacterial colony in the gravel; these bacteria will later process the nitrites released into the water.

One of the interesting features of damselfish is their highly territorial behavior. In a large enough tank with a varied arrangement of rocks and coral this should be no problem, but if new fish are introduced to a small tank with an established population of damselfish there will be some very serious territorial disputes, and smaller fish may suffer injuries.

Damselfish can be bred in the aquarium given good conditions, but the tiny young are difficult to feed unless a supply of a minute form of live food is available.

Clownfish are brightly colored, rounded

fish like the damsels, but they have the habit of living in a partnership with large sea anemones. Although anemones feed on small fish and invertebrates, clownfish are able to protect themselves by covering their bodies with a mixture of their own mucus and that produced by the anemone; the anemone is then unable to recognize the fish as prey. Some clownfish can live away from anemones, but a few species do not thrive unless they are in partnership. They lay their eggs at the base of their anemone host, and these hatch freely, but the minute young will

This delightful little fish is commonly called the humbug due to its similarity in color to a popular confection. The colors of the black-and-white damselfish, Dascyllus aruanus, *can create an interesting contrast against the vivid colors of a mature marine aquarium.*

Anemone fish such as these orange-fin Amphiprion chrysopterus *are able to live within the stinging tentacles of the anemone without injury, thanks to a protective layer of mucus on the fish's body. In the aquarium, these fish will readily form a close relationship with any suitable anemone.*

Damselfish such as this golden damselfish, Amblyglyphidoden aureus, *make ideal first fish for those just starting a marine aquarium. They are energetic, adapt well to life in captivity, and are tolerant of the fluctuations in water quality that can occur when setting up smaller aquaria.*

The emperor angelfish, Pomacanthus imperator, is frequently encountered in the aquarium trade and has become a favorite with marine fish keepers but, like all angels, this species is very sensitive to poor water quality.

feed only on microscopic plankton. This can only be provided by supplying fresh seawater very regularly. In fact, clownfish are generally less tolerant of poor water quality than damselfish, and are most content when there are frequent water changes.

The anemone hosts can be kept healthy by giving them small pieces of chopped fish. They also require very bright lighting, because they have symbiotic algae living inside them which require light to photosynthesize. Anemones, too, are happiest if the water is changed frequently.

Serranidae

This family is more familiarly known as groupers, large fish found in tropical and temperate waters. Some reach enormous sizes and can be quite tame when encountered by divers. Their bodies are solid and powerful,

with spiny fins and attractive markings. Only a few species are small enough to be kept in aquaria. They are usually very secretive, remaining hidden for long periods and only emerging when food is offered, quickly returning to their hiding places when the meal is over. Groupers can wedge themselves into crevices in coral if alarmed, but normally they just hover or swim very slowly around a small area.

Groupers' mouths are very large and have an extendible lower jaw, so they can eat pieces of fish or meat. In a community tank they will not bother other fish that are too large to gulp down, but they should not be kept with very small species.

Unfortunately, groupers are too large when mature to breed successfully in an aquarium. It is interesting, though, to speculate how they were named groupers, as one thing they can not do successfully is live together in a group.

Pomacanthinae

The Pomacanthinae—angelfish—are similar to butterfly fish (to which they are related), but they have thicker bodies and a sharp spine on the lower edge of the gill covers. They can become quite large and are

The spectacular colors on this regal angelfish, **Pygoplites diacanthus,** *make it easy to see how it got its name. It is, however, a shy species that is difficult to acclimatize to aquarium conditions.*

Although a very attractive species, the rock beauty, Holacanthus
tricolor, is a very large fish which requires a spacious aquarium.
In its native habitat on the reefs of the western Atlantic, this fish
eats sponges, so it is difficult to feed under aquarium conditions.

The colors of this adult French angel, Pomacanthus paru, *are quite different from the vivid black and yellow stripes seen on the juveniles of this species. Here the spine on the gill cover, which distinguishes angelfish from the similar butterfly fish, is clearly visible.*

beautifully colored. Angelfish are highly territorial and fight others of their own species quite aggressively, but they are usually less combative when given a cave in the coral in which to hide from time to time.

At one time the young and adults were thought to be separate species because of their completely different markings and colors. It was only through observing them in aquaria that the color changes were discovered and the relationship between these seemingly different fish realized.

This family has very exacting requirements for food, which must contain some vegetable matter, and water conditions, which must remain constant.

Acanthuridae

This family includes the surgeonfish, or tangs, which are noted for having a large, erect spine on either side of the tail. This spine is used in self-defense, and can inflict a nasty wound on the hand of an aquarist who does not use a net when handling one of these fish.

Tangs have rather thickened, oval-shaped bodies and are brightly colored. In the wild, they live in shoals, but they are unable to tolerate their own kind in an aquarium. They must be given some vegetable food in order to keep them healthy, but even with the best of diets, tangs do not to settle enough to breed in captivity.

Following page: A real supermodel of the fish world, this aptly named lipstick tang, Naso lituratus, has spectacularly well defined facial markings said to resemble makeup. These colors contrast greatly with the pale gray that covers much of the fish's body.

It is unusual to find a marine fish of only one color, but what this yellow tang, Zebrasoma flavescens, lacks in variety it certainly makes up for in sheer brilliance. A spacious aquarium containing a large shoal of these fish can create a stunning display.

An instantly recognizable sight to any hobbyist, the powder blue tang, Acanthurus leucosternon, is a common feature in most aquarium stores. Its bright colors and bold behavior make it one of the most popular marine fish kept in aquaria.

Surgeons such as this orangeband surgeonfish, Acanthurus olivaceous, are so called
because of the scalpel-like spine positioned near the tail, used for defense and
during territorial disputes with other fish.

Picasso triggerfish, Rhinecanthus aculeatus, are
excessively aggressive towards other aquarium resi-
dents and should be kept on their own. Despite this,
their greedy feeding habits, which make them ever
ready to take food from the hands of their owners,
make them very popular among marine aquarists.

The extraordinarily psychedelic markings of the clown trigger-fish, Balistoides conspicillum, *actually act as camouflage against the coral-encrusted reefs of the Indo-Pacific where this fish is normally found. In the aquarium, however, its markings make it unmistakable.*

Balistidae

Balistidae, or triggerfish, are noted for having huge heads which sometimes comprise one-third of the body length. The dorsal fin has a huge spine which can be raised and jammed against the roof of a cave to prevent the fish being pulled out by a predator. Their mouths are relatively small, but they have strong teeth and powerful jaws; they can easily nip fins, or even fingers, so they are best kept in tanks on their own. They should also be kept away from filter pipes and heater cables, as they will also nibble at these out of curiosity.

Triggerfish enjoy moving chunks of rock and coral around the tank, and, in the process, any invertebrates they find will be eaten. Because they are totally carnivorous, they need a diet of live shrimp and other hard-shelled foods.

Like the wrasse, triggerfish occasionally lie on their sides on the floor of the aquarium. In a large enough tank they will thrive and display other interesting behavior, including their strange method of swimming with undulating dorsal and anal fins and rigid bodies.

As with all triggerfish, the vivid patterns on this queen triggerfish, **Balistes vetula**, all seem to emphasize the mouth and head, which appear disproportionately large by comparison to the rest of the body. These markings advertise to potential predators that this fish is armed with a powerful set of teeth and jaws.

Ostraciontidae

This family is better known as the boxfish or cowfish; they have bodies encased in a rigid, box-like skin, with the eyes, mouth, and fins emerging through openings. They are curious, rather than attractive, because of their strange shape and awkward method of swimming, and are best kept alone because other fish tend to worry them. If threatened they release an unpleasant poison into the water which kills everything in the tank, including the boxfish.

Pufferfish and porcupine fish, which can inflate their bodies and erect spines for protection, are closely related species which can also be kept in a large tank.

This curiously shaped long-horned cowfish, Lactoria cornuta, is able to buzz around with the precision of a helicopter. The propelling force is created by coordinated undulations of both the pectoral and dorsal fins.

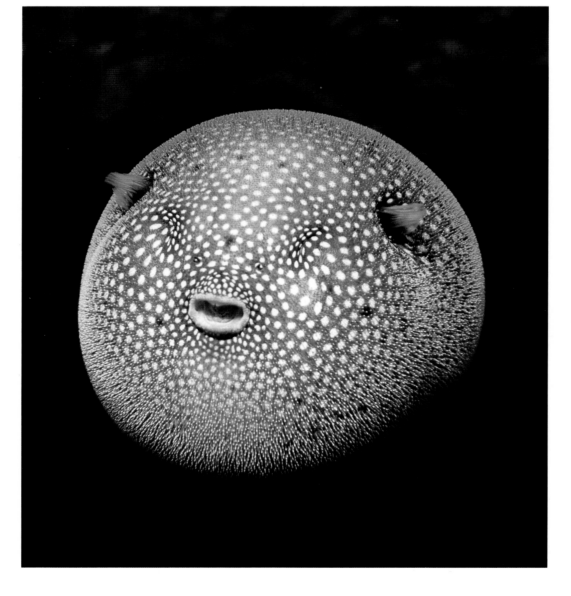

Inflating itself to bizarre proportions so that the spines on its body stand outward is this slow-moving spotted pufferfish's (Arothrodon meleagris) only means of defense. It is, however, unfair to encourage this fright response in captive animals.

The orbiculate batfish, Platax orbicularis, can reach an enormous size in the wild. In captivity this species requires a deep aquarium, but is otherwise not fussy about its diet and minor fluctuations in salinity.

INDEX

*Page numbers in **bold-face** type indicate photo captions.*